Classic Tales

Level 2

The Town Mouse and the Country Mouse

Activity Book and Play

Contents

Activities	2
Play	12
Teacher's notes	16b

Name: _____
Class: _____ School: _____

OXFORD
UNIVERSITY PRESS

Activities

Before you read, can you match the words with the pictures?

1 mouse

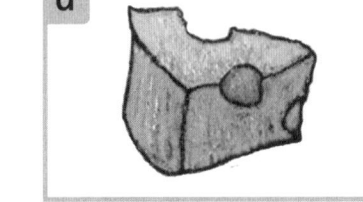 a

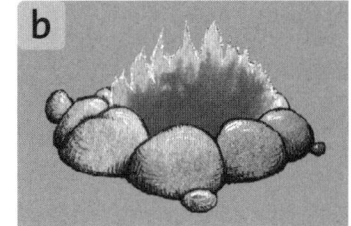 b

2 cheese

3 town

 c

 d

4 sheep

5 clock

 e

 f

6 fire

7 trousers

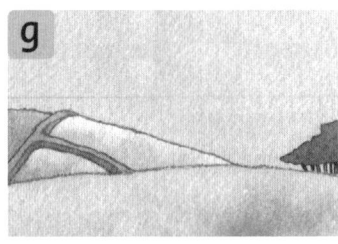 g

 h

8 country

→ Pages 2–3

1 Answer the questions.

1 Who is it? It's __Town Mouse__.
Is he in the town now? _____.
Where is he? He's in the _____.

2 Who is it? It's _____.
Who comes to see him? _____.
Does Town Mouse eat a lot? _____.

2 Circle the correct words. Then complete the sentences.

1 Town Mouse is Country Mouse's ___friend___.
   brother (friend) father
2 One day he comes to Country Mouse's _____.
   home school shop
3 There's a lot to _____.
   do eat see
4 But Town Mouse thinks the _____ is strange.
   table room food
5 He doesn't _____ it very much.
   look at need like
6 So he only eats _____ bit.
   a little a big another

Pages 4–5

1 Circle the mistake in each sentence. Then write the correct word.

1 Town Mouse sleeps in Country Mouse's (chair). _bed_
2 Outside it's very white and quiet. _____
3 In the morning Town Mouse is happy. _____
4 But Country Mouse wants to get some money. _____

2 Put the words in the correct order.

1 Country his Mouse bed Mouse gives Town.
   Country Mouse gives Town Mouse his bed.

2 can bed You my have tonight.
   _____

3 is Country bed But strange Mouse's.
   _____

4 much like Mouse doesn't Town it very.
   _____

5 sleep can't to go He.
   _____

6 very It's quiet dark and.
   _____

7 Mouse is In tired morning the Town.
   _____

8 get go some and food Let's.
   _____

→ **Pages 6–7**

Write the words. Then complete the sentences.

a

b

t e e f _____feet_____   a r s g s _____

c    d

o t w n _____   c w o _____

e 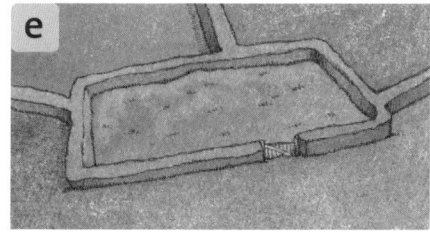   f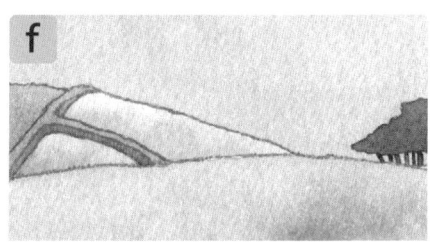

i f e d l _____   y o c n u r t _____

1 The _____ is long and wet.
2 Town Mouse's _feet_ and trousers are wet.
3 He doesn't like the _____ very much!
4 There's a cow in the _____ .
5 'It's only a _____ !' laughs Country Mouse.
6 Town Mouse says, 'I think I like the _____ best.'

5

→ Pages 8–9

1 What does Town Mouse say? Circle the correct words.

'I like the town **a little** / **better**.
It's **bad** / **nice** and **warm** / **cold** and
dry / **wet** in the **country** / **town**. It isn't
cold / **dark** at **night** / **home** and there's
a lot / **everything** to **see** / **buy**. It's very
quiet / **interesting**. And **it's** / **there's** a
lot of **water** / **food**! Let's go **there** / **here**.
Come **with** / **near** me and **help** / **see**.'

2 Answer the questions.

1 What are they?
They are _____sheep_____.
What does the man say to them?
'_____ up!'

2 What is it? It's a _____.
Where is it going?
It's _____.

3 What are they?
They are two _____.
Does Town Mouse want to go in
the cart? _____.

→ **Pages 10–11**

1 Write the words. Match the pictures with the sentences.

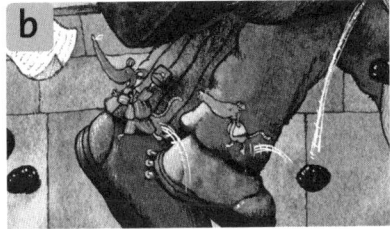

here ~~town~~ clock people

1 [b] Town Mouse and Country Mouse are in the __town__ .
2 [ ] There are a lot of _____ .
3 [ ] The _____ makes a strange noise.
4 [ ] Town Mouse lives _____ .

2 Write the words.

~~Soon~~ much only happily Suddenly

1 __Soon__ Town Mouse is home.
2 'It's good to be home again,' he says, _____ .
3 Country Mouse doesn't like the big house very _____ .
4 _____ there is a strange noise.
5 'It's _____ the clock,' laughs Town Mouse.

7

→ **Pages 12–13**

Choose a, b, or c.

1 There's a lot to …
   a ✓ eat   b ☐ drink   c ☐ see
2 But Country Mouse thinks the food is …
   a ☐ nice   b ☐ warm   c ☐ strange
3 He doesn't like it …
   a ☐ today   b ☐ now   c ☐ very much
4 Country Mouse only eats …
   a ☐ a lot   b ☐ a little bit   c ☐ everything
5 Town Mouse says, 'Please have …'
   a ☐ another   b ☐ some more   c ☐ anything
6 'No thank you,' … Country Mouse.
   a ☐ says   b ☐ thinks   c ☐ asks
7 Town Mouse gives Country Mouse his …
   a ☐ food   b ☐ clock   c ☐ bed
8 He says, 'You can have my bed …'
   a ☐ tonight   b ☐ today   c ☐ now
9 But Country Mouse can't go to …
   a ☐ town   b ☐ school   c ☐ sleep
10 It isn't … in the room.
   a ☐ cold   b ☐ dark   c ☐ hot
11 The … is very noisy.
   a ☐ street   b ☐ cart   c ☐ clock

→ **Pages 14–15**

1 **Write the words and number the sentences 1–7.**

cat   food   ~~tired~~   mice   trap   away   cheese

a ☐ At last the cat goes _____ .
b ☐ Town Mouse says, 'Let's go and get some _____ .'
c [1] In the morning Country Mouse is ___tired___ .
d ☐ Town Mouse shouts, 'It's a _____ !'
e ☐ But there's a _____ and they can't go out.
f ☐ Suddenly, Country Mouse sees some _____ .
g ☐ Now the two _____ are very hungry.

2 **Answer the questions.**

1 Who is it?
It's _Town Mouse_ .
Is he tired? _____ .
What does he want to go and get?
Some _____ .
Are the mice very thirsty?
No, they _____ .

2 What is it?
It's _____ .
Does Country Mouse want to eat it? _____ .

3 What is it?
It's a _____ .
What does Town Mouse shout?
'STOP! _____ that!'

→ **Pages 16–17**

1 **Put the words in the correct order. Who is speaking? Write *Town Mouse* or *Country Mouse*.**

   1 the Do town like you?
   Do you like the town? _Town Mouse_

   2 strange very It's here.

   3 best think I the like I country.

   4 good the is in Life town.

   5 country better I like But the.

   6 and quiet nice country in It's the.

   7 We things different like.

2 **What does Country Mouse say about the town and the country? Write the words. Then choose.**

   It's …

		The town	The country
1 g e a t s n r	s_trange_	✓	☐
2 q t e u i	q_____	☐	☐
3 n e g n i s t r e t i	i_____	☐	☐
4 i f r d e f e n t	d_____	☐	☐
5 e c i n	n_____	☐	☐

10

→ **Pages 18–19**

1 **What do they say? Write the words.**

1 Hurry _up, you children_ .

2 That _____ to the country.

3 _____ me.

2 **Find and circle the words. Then complete the sentences.**

d	x	c	a	r	t	j	k
r	n	s	z	f	i	r	e
i	w	b	m	l	h	q	f
v	g	o	o	d	o	v	r
e	v	q	z	b	m	g	i
r	y	e	c	x	e	k	e
c	o	u	n	t	r	y	n
p	i	j	k	v	z	t	d

1 The next day they see a ___cart___ .
2 It's going to the _____ .
3 'Hurry up, you children,' says the _____ .
4 'Goodbye, my _____ ,' says Country Mouse.
5 Soon Country Mouse is _____ .
6 He sits by the _____ .
7 'It's _____ to be home again,' he says.

Play

Act the play.

> **Characters**
>
>  Chorus    Town Mouse
>
>  Country Mouse    Man

→ Pages 2–3   🍃 **Scene 1** 🍃

Chorus: One day Town Mouse comes to see Country Mouse.

Town Mouse: Hello, Country Mouse!
Country Mouse: Hello, my friend!

Chorus: There's a lot to eat. But Town Mouse doesn't like the food very much. So he only eats a little bit.

Country Mouse: Please have some more.
Town Mouse: It's very nice, but no thank you.

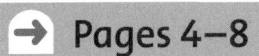 Pages 4–8

Scene 2

Country Mouse: You can have my bed tonight.
Town Mouse: Thank you.
Chorus: But Town Mouse can't go to sleep.
It's very dark and quiet.

Scene 3

Chorus: In the morning Town Mouse is tired.
But Country Mouse isn't tired.

Country Mouse: Let's go and get some food.
Town Mouse: Oh! What's that?
Country Mouse: It's only a cow!

Scene 4

Country Mouse: Do you like the country?
Town Mouse: It's different. But I think I like the town best.
Country Mouse: Life is good in the country.
Town Mouse: Yes. But I like the town better.
It's interesting. Come with me and see.

→ Pages 9–12

Scene 5

Chorus: The next day the two mice see a cart.

Man: Hurry up, you sheep! I want to go to town.
Town Mouse: That cart's going to town. Come on.

Scene 6

Town Mouse: Ah! It's good to be home again.
Country Mouse *(quietly)*: What a lot of people!

Chorus: The house is big. Country Mouse doesn't like it very much. Suddenly there is a strange noise.

Country Mouse: Oh! What's that?
Town Mouse: It's only the clock. Look! I live there. Let's go and eat. Come on!

Scene 7

Chorus: There's a lot to eat. But Country Mouse doesn't like the food very much.

Town Mouse: Please have some more.
Country Mouse: It's very nice, but no thank you.

→ Pages 13–15

Scene 8

Town Mouse: You can have my bed tonight.
Country Mouse: Thank you.

Chorus: But Country Mouse can't go to sleep. It isn't dark in the room and the street is very noisy.

Scene 9

Chorus: In the morning Country Mouse is tired. But Town Mouse isn't tired.

Town Mouse: Come on! Let's go and get some food.

Chorus: But there's a cat and they can't go out.

Scene 10

Chorus: At last the cat goes away. The two mice are very hungry. Suddenly Country Mouse sees something.

Country Mouse: Look! Cheese!
Town Mouse: STOP! Don't touch that! It's a trap!

→ Pages 16–19   ## Scene 11

Town Mouse: Do you like the town?

Country Mouse: It's different. But I think I like the country best.

Town Mouse: Life is good in the town.

Country Mouse: Yes. But I like the country better. It's nice and quiet in the country.

Town Mouse: I understand. We like different things.

Scene 12

Chorus: The next day they see a cart.

Man: Hurry up, you children. I want to go to the country.

Country Mouse: That cart's going to the country. Goodbye, my friend. Thank you.

Town Mouse: Write to me.

Chorus: Soon Country Mouse is home. He sits by the fire.

Country Mouse: Ah! It's good to be home again.

The End